How to SURVIVE a Quarter-life CRISIS

HOW TO SURVIVE A QUARTER-LIFE CRISIS

Text and illustrations by Anna Martin
Additional text by Hannah Adams

An Hachette UK Company
www.hachette.co.uk

Summersdale Publishers Ltd
Part of Octopus Publishing Group Limited
Carmelite House
50 Victoria Embankment
LONDON
EC4Y 0DZ
UK

www.summersdale.com

Printed and bound in the Czech Republic

ISBN: 978-1-78783-007-3

Substantial discounts on bulk quantities of Summersdale books are available to corporations, professional associations and other organizations. For details contact general enquiries: telephone: +44 (0) 1243 771107 or email: enquiries@summersdale.com.

How to SURVIVE a Quarter-life CRISIS

I'M CUTE but PSYCHO

Successful career

Fulfilling relationship

SKINNY

Decaf

HATTIE HAMILTON

ILLUSTRATIONS BY ANNA MARTIN

summersdale

TO............................

FROM............................

CONTENTS

INTRODUCTION   9

Ten Signs You're Having a Quarter-Life Crisis   10

Quarter-Life Crisis Toolkit   14

CAREER   19

Umm, Excuse Me, Where's My Career?   20

Why Dead-End Jobs Are Good for You   24

25 Most Disappointing Under 25   27

The Art of the Quarter-Life Side Hustle   32

How to Survive (and Maybe
Even Enjoy) Internships   36

VIRTUAL LIFE   39

It's Good to Share – But Try Not to Overshare   42

What Type of Social Media User Are You?   44

How to Break Up with Social Media   48

LOVE   51

Why Haven't I Found "the One"?   52

Why Modern Love Is Like Netflix   58

Where to Look vs Where Not to Look for
"the One"   62

Love Songs for Your Quarter-Life Crisis   70

Not Defined by Love   72

FRIENDSHIPS AND REAL LIFE 75

The Five Types of Friend in a
Quarter-Life Crisis 76

Hang Out with People Older (or Younger)
Than You 78

Living in a Shared House 80

Some Quality Comebacks for the
School Reunion 84

"I'm Not Living the Dream — I'm Living
at Home!" 88

Quarter-Life Coffee 91

LIFESAVERS 97

Crafting Through Your Quarter-Life Crisis 98

A List of Films to Help You Through the Dark
Times of Your Quarter-Life Crisis 102

Meditate the Sh*t Out of Your
Quarter-Life Crisis! 104

Help Others 108

The Sabbatical 112

Travel Tips for a Quarter-Life Sabbatical 114

FINAL THOUGHTS 118

Ten Commandments for the Quarter-Lifer 120

MIC DROP 124

INTRODUCTION

Are you feeling stressed, confused and found wanting in this world of supposed endless possibilities? Then you're not alone. A study of twenty- and thirty-somethings conducted by LinkedIn in 2018 discovered that over 70 per cent had experienced a quarter-life crisis, and over 30 per cent are currently experiencing one.

The struggle is real; out of nowhere, you suddenly feel the pressures of securing a career, earning good money (or at least enough to live on), getting onto the housing ladder and finding lasting love, all while maintaining that Insta-rosy glow on your social media. How has anyone successfully managed to navigate this endless maze of adulthood?

Rest assured, this book will carefully guide you through the choppy waters of your quarter-life crisis. With advice on how to find love without losing your mind, ways to build your skill set in a dead-end job, tips for coping with a filthy housemate and much more, you will soon be winning at life again.

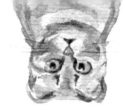

TEN SIGNS YOU'RE HAVING A QUARTER-LIFE CRISIS

1. *You continually find yourself asking what your purpose in life is.*

2. *You can't decide if you want to be treated like an adult or mothered like a small child.*

3. *Your anxiety skyrockets when scrolling through the endless engagement and pregnancy posts from your friends on social media.*

4. *You spend most of your day fantasizing about living your cat's life.*

5. *You're 99.5 per cent sure that backpacking across Asia would fix your problems.*

6. *You buy branded items of clothing to convince yourself that you're not cripplingly broke.*

7. *You feel like a failure for still living at home or in a shared house (but a part of you is relieved you don't have to worry about even more bills and responsibilities).*

8. *You'd literally spend your last penny on a moment of clarity.*

9. *You now accept that you possess none of the answers. To be honest, you're not even sure what the questions are.*

10. *You picked up this book.*

If you said yes to any of these points, it's official: you're having a quarter-life crisis. But, fear not – you're in the right place at the right time. Here is your life raft and comfort blanket rolled into one sweet package, which will help you to weather even the stormiest quarter-life crisis.

MY "LIFE GOALS BEFORE 25" WHEN I WAS 20:

have a mortgage, become a CEO or social media sensation, have good hair, have my own sustainable coffee shop, travel to 98 countries.

MY LIFE GOALS ON THE EVE OF MY TWENTY-FIFTH BIRTHDAY:

afford my rent without getting overdrawn this month, get at least two likes on my Instagram post of my new shoes, remember to pluck nose hairs before work, stop mislaying my refillable coffee cup, visit my parents once a month.

QUARTER-LIFE CRISIS TOOLKIT

Let's get down to business – you're going to need to arm yourself with a few essentials to get you through your mid-twenties malaise, plus this is the best excuse you'll have all year to buy a large tote bag to lug your crisis kit around! Here are some essentials:

A craft of your choice (see page 98) – just to keep those idle hands busy so you're not constantly reaching for your phone. It's the best way to banish those FOMO feelings.

A "Why I'm Great" journal (which you can keep adding to) for noting down what makes you awesome – it's something to dip into when you're feeling like a pile of sh*t. Go one better and have a mighty fine selfie affixed to the cover!

Snacks – plan these for the week ahead and hide them in the deepest recesses of your pockets, bags and dungarees, like sweet little surprises for future you. Fuelling up during a quarter-life crisis is essential, so you might as well make your taste buds tingle.

A charm or talisman to hold when you're feeling jittery, such as when you have a meeting at the bank or a job interview. Maybe don't bring your teddy or worry beads along for these appointments, but a crystal or small item of jewellery you can wear is ideal.

A smartphone but with timed access to social media. Think of social media like the hottest hottie ever but with a disgusting habit like picking their nose and eating it. It's fine in really small doses – you can look and admire for a bit – but after that, eugh.

Something that makes your heart go boom! This could be anything, from an image of your dream pet or next holiday destination to an article on resilience that makes you go "F*ck yeah!" It'll keep you going when you really, desperately want to tell your boss to stick it.

Copies of your CV – because you never know whom you're going to meet.

Headphones – to play those QLC tunes (see page 70).

Reusable coffee cup – need I explain?

Career

QUARTER-LIFE CRISIS, STEP ONE:

When you realize you are at least a decade
behind on your dream career path and you
question your purpose in life on a daily basis.

UMM, EXCUSE ME, WHERE'S MY CAREER?

You've worked hard (well, mostly) and earned a degree or diploma, with a debt the size of Kim K's derrière to show for it, and you find yourself asking "What now?" To the untrained eye you have it all – youth and beauty, good health, an education, maybe even a great collection of vintage flares – but what are you meant to do with it all? It's like having all the ingredients for a showstopper but no method to combine them into something truly satisfying. You've got so much to give, but where or what do you give it to? It's enough to make you weep into that RIXO tea dress you couldn't really afford.

While our parents appeared to skip from education to a good job and a mortgage in one seemingly faultless movement, the quarter-lifer of today has to make like Katniss just to get a foot on any rung, let alone all

I COULDN'T LIVE WITHOUT IT...

of them. Accepting that forging a career is a process with many machinations will help you to think positively. Lower your expectations in the first instance; aim for small steps in your career trajectory rather than giant leaps. Be in it for the long haul, not the instant gains, and, above all, don't compare yourself to the lucky bastard from your year who has nabbed their dream job – being at the perceived "top" isn't always golden, even if their feed would suggest otherwise.

Use your natural charm and friends, family, tutors and the mighty internet to build a network of contacts. Seek advice from those in the industries that you want to become a part of and see if they offer work placements – learn the reality of your chosen profession, not the fantasy. Keep knocking on that door, and one day it will open.

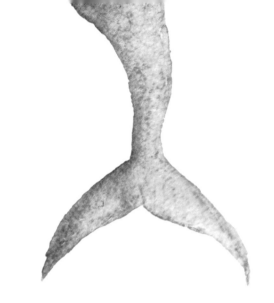

WHY DEAD-END JOBS
ARE GOOD FOR YOU

Working in a dead-end job can sometimes feel like a living nightmare of interminable drudgery and gloom, but it's comforting to remember that 99.9 per cent of the population experience this life-sap at some stage in their lives. While you feel your drive and enthusiasm slowly drain away like that lukewarm soy latte you forgot to drink, keep in mind that even the most tedious jobs have value.

Whether the job you're doing is the bottom rung on the ladder leading toward your career goal or you're simply shovelling metaphorical sh*t, take note of the skills you are racking up for when you one day move on to far, far better things.

It might also help to remember that no job is perfect – not even the one you've been dreaming of since you were five and told everyone about at Show and Tell. So, make sure you take this opportunity to master the arts of tolerance and admin.

Also, bear in mind that your job isn't your whole life! Sure, it might take up a large chunk of your waking hours, but think about all those hours that you're free. As you're using your day job to pay the bills and save toward that thousand-dollar mono-fin so you can be a real-life mermaid, use your free time to do something more relevant to your future career or personal fulfilment. Working on a voluntary basis at the weekends or for a charity you care about in the evenings is a great way not only to get more out of your time but also to bolster your CV for your next job application.

If nothing else, working in a dead-end job is going to teach you some powerful lessons – namely what things you definitely do not enjoy doing (and, if you're lucky, some things that you do). And when you do eventually fulfil that dream of handing in your notice, you can do so knowing that any job you go to next will feel like absolute paradise.

AND YOU MAKE A GREAT EASTER BUNNY. JUST TRY NOT TO SCOWL.

25 MOST DISAPPOINTING UNDER 25

In the age of social media, when we are constantly connected to the virtual world, it's easier than ever to feel totally inadequate. After all, we all know of a 15-year-old Instagram influencer who is making more money than most of us will see in a lifetime. But while we often make role models of those young, beautiful few who have somehow achieved #lifegoals before you feel like you've even started, there are so many inspirational people who found success much later in life. And, you'll soon realize, it really doesn't matter how you started out.

SAMUEL L. JACKSON

Grew up with a stutter, which he was bullied for, and started using the word "motherf*cker" as an affirmation.

STEPHEN KING

Had his first book, *Carrie*, rejected 30 times.

SYLVESTER STALLONE
Found himself on the brink of homelessness and sold his pet dog to stay afloat.

SIDNEY POITIER
Messed up his first theatre audition and was told to get a job washing dishes instead.

THOMAS EDISON
Told during school that he was "too stupid to learn anything".

ALAN RICKMAN
Decided at 18 years old that drama school wasn't a sensible career path, so he worked as a graphic designer instead.

WALT DISNEY
Fired from a newspaper because his editor felt he "lacked imagination and had no good ideas".

OPRAH WINFREY
Publicly fired from her first TV job as an anchor for getting too emotionally invested in her stories.

STEVEN SPIELBERG
Rejected by the University of Southern California School of Cinematic Arts on multiple occasions.

ISAAC NEWTON

Pulled out of school by his mother to run the family farm.

VERA WANG

Failed to make the US Olympics figure-skating team, and worked as a journalist through most of her young life.

STAN LEE

Worked multiple part-time jobs while he was growing up, including as an obituary writer, a delivery boy and a store clerk.

CHARLES DARWIN

He was regarded by his tutors as "average". He also preferred riding and shooting to studying for his BA at Cambridge.

J. K. ROWLING

Seven years after graduating from university, Rowling saw herself as a failure; she was jobless and her marriage had broken down, leaving her a single mother.

MADONNA

Dropped out of college, moved to New York and took a job at Dunkin' Donuts in Times Square, where she was fired after one day.

ELVIS PRESLEY

Told by a concert hall manager that he was better off returning to Memphis and driving trucks.

MARILYN MONROE

Told by modelling agencies early in her career that she should consider becoming a secretary.

MICHAEL JORDAN

Cut from his high-school basketball team.

RUDYARD KIPLING

Fired from his editorial job in his early twenties after being told that he "didn't know how to use the English language".

LISA KUDROW

Cast as Roz on the TV show *Frasier* and fired two days into rehearsals.

THEODOR SEUSS GEISEL (DR SEUSS)

Had his first children's book rejected by more than 20 publishers.

KATY PERRY

Dropped out of high school to pursue a career in singing and was dropped by three major record labels.

BILL GATES
Dropped out of Harvard and was the co-owner of failed business Traf-O-Data.

BARBRA STREISAND
Made her debut on the New York stage with a show that opened and closed on the same night.

VINCENT VAN GOGH
Sold one painting during his life.

See, everyone goes through setbacks, but the secret is to keep going!

THE ART OF THE QUARTER-LIFE SIDE HUSTLE

When your job isn't your jam and you need more bread, just make a jam sandwich! It's time to join the 50 per cent who hustle on the side. Just to clear a few things up: it has nothing to do with shooting pool with gangsters or supplying contraband (although I can't speak for everyone). It's basically something you do outside of your regular job that makes money. It's a way to raise extra cash doing something you enjoy that you can potentially develop into a full-blown career. Quarter-life is the optimum time for building a side-hustle empire and becoming a "slashie" (artist/muse/bouncer/whatever).

Limit the hours you spend on your side hustle in the first instance – you don't want it to become a chore – then gradually build up the time incrementally as you see fit. Instead of binge-watching Netflix after work every day, use this time to get hustlin'!

SELLING

Be it a product or a service, selling something is the most obvious way to go. Etsy, eBay and Amazon open up the whole world in terms of selling things – from crafts to vintage finds. Perhaps you have a great eye and can spot the gems among the trash in a jumble sale? Your passion can now pay for itself and maybe afford you a little holiday, too.

SKILL SHARE

Whether it's coding, baking or guitar lessons, use your skills and share them, either in an online capacity, in one-to-ones or as part of a group.

BLOGGING

If writing is your thing, start a blog.

MISC.

Like dogs? Offer dog-walking services. Love driving? Offer lifts to people you know in return for payment. Love gardening? Offer to spruce up a few gardens in the neighbourhood on a regular basis. Love escape rooms? Create your own in your house!* You get the gist, and the money will soon roll in!

*Use your common sense, please!

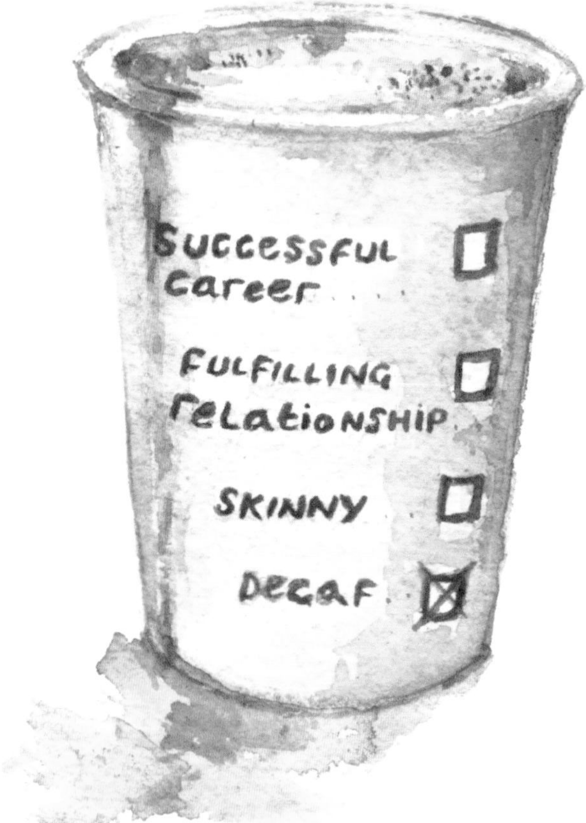
Successful career
Fulfilling relationship
Skinny
Decaf

#QUARTERLIFEGOALS

Where am I going with this? I should have my life sorted by now. Taylor Swift was so sorted at 22 that she wrote a song about it.

Positive takeaway: At least you're on decaf now.

HOW TO SURVIVE (AND MAYBE EVEN ENJOY) INTERNSHIPS

Despite being told your whole life that you would walk straight into the job of your dreams "if only you believed", it is now quite clear that life has not panned out for you in this rose-tinted way. In fact, so far from the truth is this that you've actually found yourself without any job at all (even one at the local burger chain, who rejected your application because of your "lack of experience" – are they for real?).

So, the time has come for you to enter the world of work voluntarily (as in, without payment), in the form of work experience.

You may have heard horror stories from your friends about being forced to make tea all day or filing documents until their brain turned to mush and, well, these stories are all true. So here are some tips for surviving your own work experience:

- Master the art of tea and coffee making before you arrive, so that when you're inevitably given the role of Official Hot Beverage Maker, you'll ace every round.

- Speak to as many people as possible. It might seem intimidating at first, but networking will be invaluable to you if you ever apply to join the company on a permanent basis. And you'll learn loads about the industry while you're at it.

- Make a good impression. This doesn't mean you need to do something outrageous to get noticed, but do try to go the extra mile when you're given a task, so that you mark yourself out from the countless other bright young things that pass through their doors. Or ply people with copious biscuits and cakes. That also helps.

Above all, try to enjoy yourself. You never know what might come out of it!

Virtual Life

QUARTER-LIFE CRISIS, STEP TWO:

When you start to question your place in the virtual world, never mind the real one.

#QUARTERLIFEGOALS

I guess I can squeeze in an hour or two of overanalyzing every social media post before I go to sleep.

Positive takeaway: Make the most of those sleepless nights by practising your selfie face (or just your resting bitch face).

IT'S GOOD TO SHARE – BUT TRY NOT TO OVERSHARE

Unless you have the hide of a rhino, be selective about what you send out into the digital universe – this includes everyone with internet access, which is approximately 55 per cent of the whole damn world!

You may feel like you're having a good hair day, but there will always be haters out there. The 58 trolls who think your locks are a bit greasy or that you've photoshopped the highlights are just trying to bait you and bring you down.

If you know you look good, you don't need validation from a bunch of faceless strangers that you'll never, ever meet IRL.

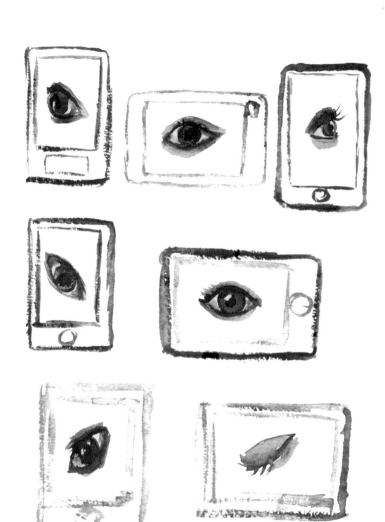

43

WHAT TYPE OF SOCIAL MEDIA USER ARE YOU?

They say it takes all sorts to make a world, so it's no surprise that the world of social media contains a truly *vast* array of personalities. Whether you identify with one, three or all of the "people" below, you're bound to exhibit these behaviours at least once in your social media career.

THE OVER-SHARER

This person loves social media so much that you can't remember the last time your feed wasn't full with their posts. Whether they're spamming everyone with a daily breakfast pic or making an Insta story about changing a broken lightbulb, they have an unquenchable thirst for attention and likes – just don't feed it, or they'll never stop.

THE SILENT SCROLLER

Occasionally, you genuinely forget that this person exists online. Having seamlessly blended themselves into the social media crowd, the only reminder of their online existence is the fact that sometimes other people tag them in a photo or mention them in a comment. With their ninja-level scrolling, they may have a future in espionage.

THE TRAVELLER

Seriously, is this person ever not on holiday? Seems like every day they're jetting off to a new exotic destination or have found another gloriously sunny location to stage a good "hot dogs or legs?" pic. They may provide you with some serious travel inspo – but you often just sit and wonder how on earth they are able to fund their wanderlust.

THE KEYBOARD ACTIVIST

This person sees social media merely as a vessel for the effective distribution of information to their followers and friends. They have fingers poised on

their keyboard ready to fight their next online battle, but you wonder if they have the balls to take their fight into the real world. You also wonder if they ever truly relax...

There's a reason social media is full of cute cat videos and puppy posts – this person right here. Whether it's their own pet, or an animal they have spotted out in the street, they absolutely have to share it with the online world. This person is solely responsible for the cute and fluffy quotient on your social media, and honestly, we love them for it.

HOW TO BREAK UP WITH SOCIAL MEDIA

Social media is our generation's blessing – and also its curse. It seems strange that something invented to make us feel more connected has somehow made us all feel more alone. And like any toxic relationship, even though we all know how bad it is for us, we feel like we can't possibly live without it. It's high time we told social media who's boss and live our lives without seeking its constant and poisonous validation.

STEP ONE: CUT DOWN

While some people might have the supernatural willpower to go cold turkey on their favourite social media sites, the rest of us mere mortals may need to take baby steps to get there. Try cutting down your social media time day by day, gradually decreasing the amount of time you spend scrolling, until you're down to almost nothing. A good start is to turn off your notifications, so the constant reminder to keep up with your socials is removed.

STEP TWO: SHUT DOWN

Let's face it; as long as you have the app staring brightly up at you when you open your phone, the temptation to click on it is going to be too strong. Once you've got to the point where you're spending a very small portion of your day on your favourite site, take the plunge and delete the app from your phone. If you usually go straight to the webpage, then set this up on your phone as a restricted website.

STEP THREE: PUT DOWN

Once you've completed these first two steps, you might be asking yourself what on earth you're going to do with all those hours you used to spend scrolling through nonsensical cat memes and pictures of your frenemies on idyllic sandy beaches. This is the best part: put down your phone and live life distraction-free. Without the crutch of cracking out your phone at every quiet spell, you'll begin to feel genuinely present in the moment

and appreciate the smaller things going on around you. In fact, with all the time you now have, you can use it to focus on a side hustle. You never know where your new hobbies might take you.

Love

QUARTER-LIFE CRISIS, STEP THREE:

Question whether The One actually
exists, and if they do, wonder
where the bloody hell they are.

WHY HAVEN'T I FOUND "THE ONE"?

The Big L, the mothership, and, if you're a literary quarter-lifer with a stack of Brontës and Austens to your name, well, there's no hope. Or is there? If you're expecting Mr Darcy or Miss Bennet to stride out of the digital cesspool of online dating sites, you're in for a rude awakening. Finding love can feel exhausting – a 24/7 job when you're constantly checking apps, texts and tweets for The One to pop up on your screen like that once-in-a-lifetime shoe sale, only to discover they don't have your size. Here are a few reminders when it comes to navigating love online.

VALUE YOURSELF

Don't be tempted to put it all out there – whether that involves a sultry pose or too much information about your preference for firefighters or mermaids. Anyone and everyone will have access to what you put up, including potential employers and your uncle George. Also,

it's important to keep something back for when you eventually meet someone you actually like.

BE NICE, BUT NOT TOO NICE

Don't write cheques your heart can't cash! It's lovely to give and receive compliments, but once again, hold back, or you could sound inauthentic and maybe even a bit desperate.

BE HONEST

It's tempting to post an older photo or even tell a few little white lies about your occupation to make you seem more attractive, but lying is the worst possible way to begin a relationship. It could get more complicated than the plot of *Inception* as you try to explain who those oldies milling around your house are when you've said you're single with a mortgage but you're actually living with your parents.

STRANGER DANGER!

There's no need to reiterate the pitfalls of communicating with strangers, online or in real life. We all start off as strangers before becoming friends or beginning a relationship, but don't mistake those

cute texts for something more meaningful when they're from someone with a dodgy nickname whom you've only seen in a posed photograph. Use online dating as a means to expand your social network and don't push for a relationship – you don't get more points depending on how many dates you've had. Just enjoy the journey and stay safe.

HAVE AN ESCAPE PLAN

You've exchanged flirty messages for a few weeks and made some serendipitous connections (you both want to hike Kilimanjaro and own a cockapoo someday). But when you're sitting in a café on a wet Sunday afternoon opposite someone who has spent the first 15 minutes of the date telling you about their stamp collection,  and they have an annoying habit of dipping their finger in the sugar bowl, you need to make a dignified exit. Plan for a bad date, whether that's by tapping up the server to announce your taxi has arrived and it's parked around the corner, or arranging for a friend to ring you 20 minutes in to tell you they're on fire. You'll thank yourself later.

GO DUTCH

This is the twenty-first century; you're independent and you can pay half the bill.

Oh, and don't google your potential sweetheart, if you can help it – keep the mystery alive!

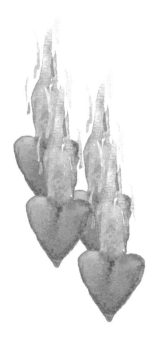

#QUARTERLIFEGOALS

I've been breadcrumbed, catfished, birdboxed and orbited – now all I want is a non-psycho to eat a takeaway with, who likes my taste in gothic-indie films. Is that asking too much?

WHY MODERN LOVE IS LIKE NETFLIX

Have you ever slumped on your bed, longing to watch something that will give you a lift, only to open Netflix and be faced with a flood of options that you have to spend hours filtering through to find something that fulfils your every desire at that precise moment in time? If so, then you'll also be familiar with the woes of modern love.

Whoever said you can't have too much of a good thing clearly never had Netflix. Or online dating apps. Because, let's face it, gone are the days when you'd stroll into the dance hall and get swept off your feet by your future lover. Nowadays, dating apps rule the romantic scene. And just like choosing the perfect Netflix series, first you've got to choose the perfect dating app to start your love story.

But the choices don't stop there. Once you're set up, you have to spend hours filtering

through hundreds of profiles and battling to figure out how much you're going to like this total stranger.

And say you manage to choose someone among the barrage of options. Then, much like you must resist the temptation of reading up on the entire plot of the Netflix series you're watching after the first episode, you must resist searching for everything about this person online like the modern-day Miss Marple that you are. After all, on your first meeting, you do not want to accidentally ask how their aunt Susan is doing after her operation.

But that feeling when you finally find The One? They'll pull you in like that amazing series you watched in one almighty binge. And if you learned anything from that ten-season Netflix series of twelve 60-minute episodes, it's that you are a Queen of Commitment.

WHERE TO LOOK vs WHERE NOT TO LOOK FOR "THE ONE"

OK, so this is for the singletons on a dating-app embargo. Perhaps your profile went viral because of your interest in small, furry creatures, or someone highlighted something suspicious in the background of your profile picture and you've said till you're blue in the face that it's just an overripe banana. It's alright; you can do dating the old-fashioned way.

This will make you feel better. Write a list of positive things about checking your feeds every five minutes.

1.

2.

3.

4.

5.

It's a short list, isn't it? Put your phone away and experience the real life that's right in front of you. Yep, it's time to do a Mary Poppins and sing and dance your way to love in glorious technicolour. Finding your mate to samba through life with IRL might be a little slower, and with fewer pop-ups (ooh-err), but it's raw, it's fresh and it smells better than a hot smartphone.

Make a spidergram of the perfect partner and by doing so you will discover where they hang out. Turn the page to find an example, and then you can fill in your own on the pages after that.

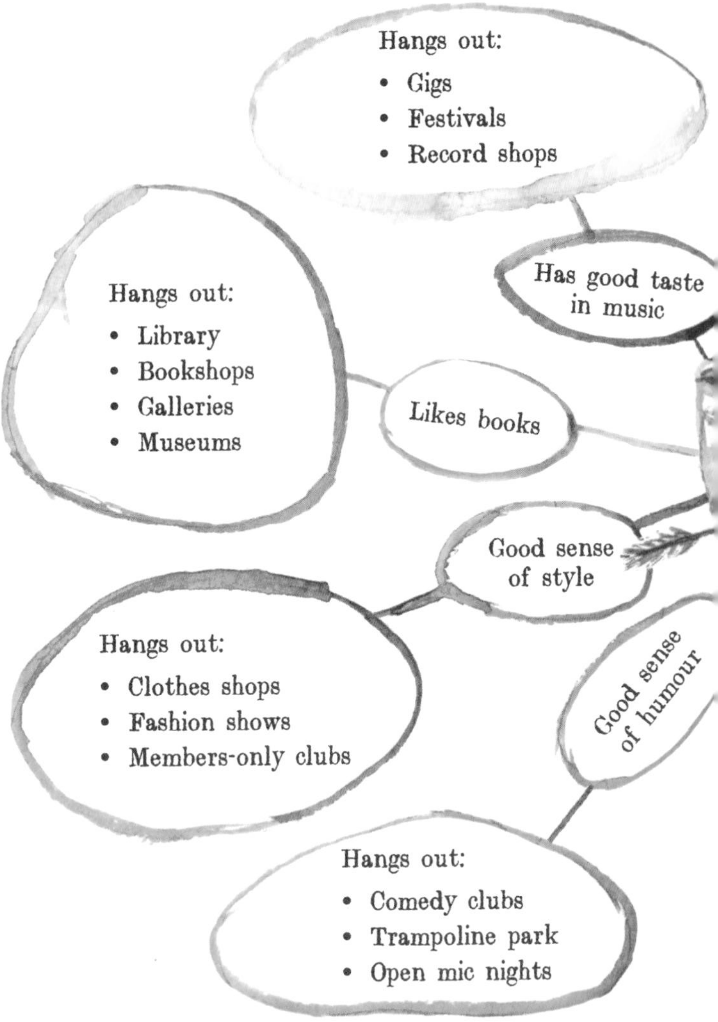

Hangs out:
- Gigs
- Festivals
- Record shops

Has good taste
in music

Hangs out:
- Library
- Bookshops
- Galleries
- Museums

Likes books

Good sense
of style

Hangs out:
- Clothes shops
- Fashion shows
- Members-only clubs

Good sense
of humour

Hangs out:
- Comedy clubs
- Trampoline park
- Open mic nights

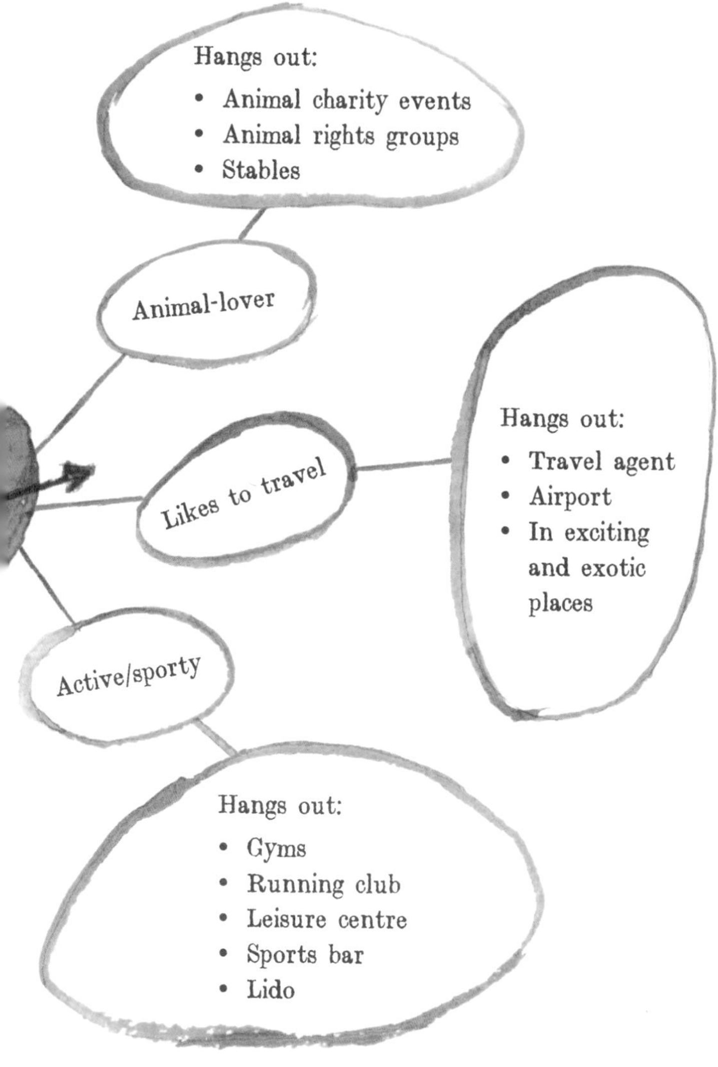

Hangs out:
- Animal charity events
- Animal rights groups
- Stables

Animal-lover

Likes to travel

Hangs out:
- Travel agent
- Airport
- In exciting and exotic places

Active/sporty

Hangs out:
- Gyms
- Running club
- Leisure centre
- Sports bar
- Lido

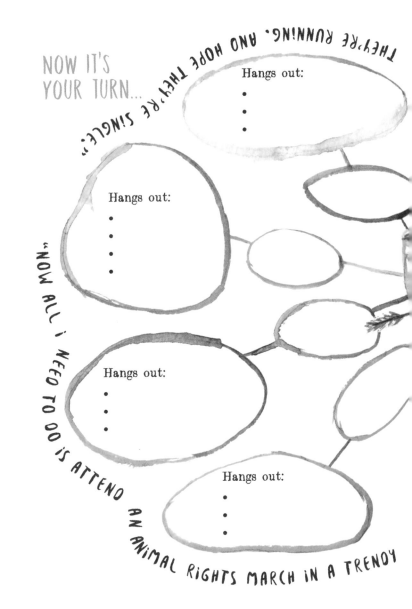

NOW IT'S YOUR TURN...

THEY'RE RUNNING, AND HOPE THEY'RE SINGLE!"

Hangs out:
•
•
•

"NOW ALL I NEED TO DO IS ATTEND AN ANIMAL RIGHTS MARCH IN A TRENDY

Hangs out:
•
•
•
•

Hangs out:
•
•
•

Hangs out:
•
•

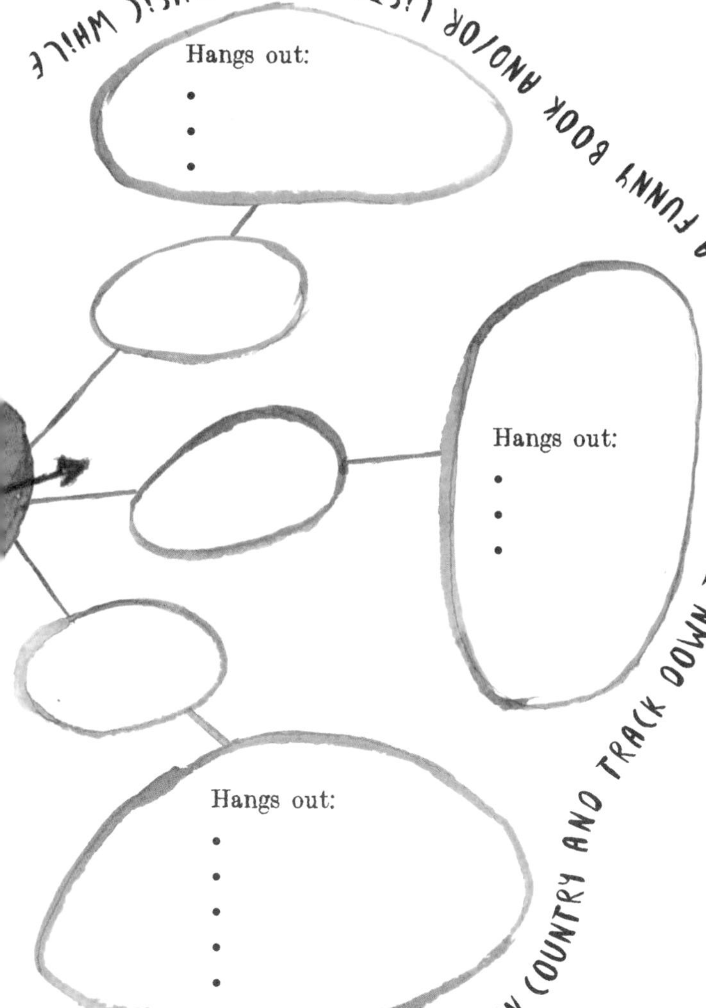

PART OF AN UNSPECIFIED FOREIGN COUNTRY AND TRACK DOWN THE PERSON READING A FUNNY BOOK AND/OR LISTENING TO MUSIC WHILE

Hangs out:
- ·
- ·
- ·

Hangs out:
- ·
- ·

Hangs out:
- ·
- ·
- ·
- ·

#QUARTERLIFEGOALS

It's not written on your face that you haven't found The One and that your track record in the love department is somewhat sketchy. It's not like you have to hawk around a relationship CV – no one will discover your sexual foibles just by meeting you in the street. Unless, of course, you're into ironic slogan tees and totes...

LOVE SONGS FOR YOUR QUARTER-LIFE CRISIS

When it's time to tear up, let it flow with these songs.

"MY HEART WILL GO ON" — CELINE DION

You were a mere nipper when this song surfaced as a soundtrack to Leo's watery demise because Kate wouldn't share the door. This rousing ballad is guaranteed to stir up something inside you, whether it's sadness or your lunch.

"LEMONADE" — BEYONCÉ

Just get it all out there, write it down and smash stuff up. See, that's better.

"TEENAGE DREAM" — KATY PERRY

This pop anthem will help you to reminisce about a time when love was all pashing and shipping. Sadly, these days, you can scroll right back to those times and see all your past mistakes in full colour. Be thankful that you're older and wiser (well, older) and you now have the skills to edit your social media feeds.

"WORK" – RIHANNA FT. DRAKE

Adjust your focus and work like a demon – it'll take your mind off the heartache.

"MAPS" – YEAH YEAH YEAHS

This charmer will remind you that you are superior in every way, and they were just plain wrong!

"i (LOVE MYSELF)" – KENDRICK LAMAR

This sunny song will help you to see the silver lining and remember that loving yourself is all that really matters.

"THANK U, NEXT" – ARIANA GRANDE

Your dating history has taught you more lessons than just pain and patience, but you're still a total girl boss and you're ready for whatever the dating world throws at you next.

NOT DEFINED
BY LOVE

Contrary to what the very rude voice in your head might say, you're not defined by love. Being single doesn't make you half a person and there's no time limit on finding love either – there's nowhere that you're uninvited or disinherited because you're not one half of a perfect couple, apart from those "couples" cruises (oh, no!). You're guaranteed to feel low if you're constantly questioning your ability to love and be loved, so try to view dating as a way to meet new friends and enjoy new experiences rather than pressuring yourself and the people you're meeting into something more.

And don't treat your singledom like a waiting room, as if you're "waiting" for your life to get interesting. Being solo is the best time to invest in yourself and discover what makes you tick, without having to consider another's feelings. You answer to nobody, and if you want to head down the Amazon in a kayak, there's no need to wait until some adventurous type sweeps you off your feet and organizes it for you. If you want to build your own house, start researching and get on with it. Plan for your own future security and make things happen. It's all there for the taking and your friends will be with you all the way – and they won't get grumpy when you're not paying them enough attention.

Friendships and Real Life

QUARTER-LIFE CRISIS, STEP FOUR:

When you realize your desperate attempts to have a social life are futile due to your permanent lack of funds.

THE FIVE TYPES
OF FRIEND IN A
QUARTER-LIFE CRISIS

THE TRIGGER (OTHERWISE KNOWN AS THE OVERACHIEVER)

Here they are – the one who started it all. This is the friend who had five internships at uni, got a mortgage at the age of 23 and now lives in the big city with their high-flying career and picture-perfect relationship. Before this friend came along, you actually thought you were doing OK. Now you spend most of your life feeling painfully left behind in every aspect of your life, from the shoes you wear, right down to your sandwich fillings – peanut butter is not cool.

THE INFLUENCER

In an age of social media, this friend has shrewdly identified the opportunity to make it big as a brunch-loving, matcha-latte-drinking, "I woke up like this" Instagram personality. Everything this friend does is plastered online, and it's impossible to even go for coffee without them whipping out their smartphone and "capturing the moment". This friend has you feeling FOMO for situations you actually attended. You now live in fear of being immortalized online in a compromising position.

THE PARTY ANIMAL

This friend is always up for a quiet drink but somehow manages to turn every occasion into an all-nighter, leading to the walk of shame as you race to work in last night's "ironic" boob tube and flares ensemble. On most nights out with this friend, you find yourself carrying them home, while they continue to cry out for just "one last drink". You may be a hot mess, but this friend can take it to a whole new level.

THE WHINGER

Everything that comes out of this friend's mouth takes the form of a complaint. Even in the moments of fleeting satisfaction, this friend knows how to find the cloud in every silver lining and make you feel ten times less optimistic than you were before. Often, they are firmly in the clutches of their own QLC, so be wary of their toxic vibes.

THE KINDRED SPIRIT

This friend is possibly the only person on earth who keeps you sane and reassures you that you're not alone in your relentless existentialism. Even when you're in the deepest darkest state of crisis, this friend is on hand with chick flicks, all the chips and dips you can eat and a listening ear. God bless the Kindred Spirit.

HANG OUT WITH PEOPLE OLDER (OR YOUNGER) THAN YOU

It's great to have fellow quarter-lifers to mope through your crisis with, but take time out to hang with the olds every now and then for a different perspective. These are the people who have survived the quarter-life crisis and have the old-school photos of bad haircuts and ill-informed lifestyle choices to prove it, but they're somehow still smiling. That's going to be you one day! You'd be surprised (maybe even horrified) by some of your older friends' stories – no one gets through the quarter-life crisis unscathed, or without some hideous inking on their arse. Give your sensible aunt a call and discover that they once mooned a coachload of pensioners and got fired from four jobs in six months – you'll start to feel like you're winning at life once more!

Conversely, hanging out with those younger than you can help you to see life from a fresh, wide-eyed viewpoint, and it gives you the perfect excuse to be a big kid again and live out those superhero fantasies. To a small child, if you're both wearing matching capes and masks, you're easily the most awesome person they've ever met. Bask in that glow and believe it, girl!

LIVING IN A
SHARED HOUSE

Ask yourself this: would you want to live with you? Living in harmony with a bunch of people who don't want to be living in a shared house is like an ongoing chemistry experiment. There are the acidic types who burn away at your soul and leave suspicious patches of goo around the place, almost like a map of their calamitous behaviour – the green stain on the carpet in front of the TV from the absinthe pong gone wrong, the burning smell whenever the oven heats up from the time when they didn't feel the need to follow instructions on a ready meal. Then there are the sub-zero types – the ones who inflict their beliefs on you. Whatever's cool at the time, that's what makes them cool. You'll never be as cool as them.

When your personality pH is different to your housemates' it can be difficult to find common ground – little and often interaction with these people will give you your best shot at domestic bliss. Here are the key points for living in a conflict-free zone.

SHARE THE CHORES

It goes without saying, doesn't it? There's no hierarchy when it comes to keeping the fridge clean and the floors vacuumed.

SHARE THE FLAWS

Everyone needs to let off steam every now and then — it's important for mental well-being not to bottle up your beef. If someone keeps leaving the toilet seat up or comes in noisily after a night out, confront them about it, but in a nice way — it'll be character-building for both of you.

SHARE THE FLOOR

Don't get all territorial in the public areas — the living room, garden, kitchen, hot tub — because no one is queen bee in a harmonious shared house.

SHUT THE DOOR

If you want alone time, keep your door closed.

#QUARTERLIFEGOALS

It's so good being in a shared house. I can see my friends whenever I want.

The bad news: when the Wi-Fi is down, you might have to talk to each other.

SOME QUALITY COMEBACKS FOR THE SCHOOL REUNION

If there's one thing more sickening than being old enough to have a school reunion, it's going to that school reunion and realizing everyone has their sh*t totally figured out. Did you somehow miss the adulting class while you were at school? Either way, here are a few conversation openers and closers to make the whole thing a little more bearable.

"You know, I still have dreams where I can't find the classroom I'm meant to be in!"

"So, what's it like actually owning a house?"

"Have you ever even used trigonometry?"

"Does anyone know why schools don't teach classes on taxes?"

"Will you support my Patreon?"

"Wow, that's so interesting, but I've just got to run to the bathroom."

"Well, your schedule sounds crazy; I won't distract you any longer!"

"This was fun; let's do it again in ten years."

"Ah, well, who am I to monopolize all your precious time!"

"It was great seeing you, but I have to go home and feed my cats."

"I'M NOT LIVING THE DREAM — I'M LIVING AT HOME!"

Living at home sounds like the dream, right? Your rent is minimal (or non-existent), your washing is done for you and you come home from work to a hot dinner on the table. Wrong. Even though you're grateful that you don't have to suffer through living in a damp flat where the heating is broken and you have to subsist on tins of cold beans to afford your extortionate rent, living with your parents in your twenties is *not* cool. So, here are a few tips to make the experience that tiny bit more bearable:

ACCEPT THAT PRIVACY IS NONEXISTENT NOW

Pri-va-cy? Who is she? Just because you might be older and (debatably) wiser, does not mean your parents see you as any different to that wayward teenager you were all those years ago. Accept that their incessant questions and unsolicited advice comes from a place of love and concern. Even if they are annoying AF.

Sure, it might seem like one of the biggest perks of living at home to have someone run around after you keeping the domestic show on the road. But even if you literally have to wrestle your dirty underwear from your parents' arms, exercising your own independence will make you feel far more in control of your life – and will serve you well once you finally fly the nest.

USE YOUR TIME (AND INCOME) WISELY

Since living at home with your parents is definitely not the dream, try to use the time and disposable income you have while living there to form your exit strategy. Saving will be easier now than it will probably ever be in future, so save up for the rent or mortgage on your own place, and at least you'll be making the best of a less-than-perfect situation.

REMEMBER YO' PRIVILEGE

It's easy to forget that actually having a warm and loving environment to call home is a luxury that many people lack. Your parents might seem like worse housemates than that kid at uni who would leave half-eaten takeaways down the back of the sofa, but you know their love will never expire (unlike those takeaways...).

And remember, living at home in your twenties is the new normal. If you're still there in your forties, then you can start to worry.

QUARTER-LIFE COFFEE

Coffee is as important as your five-a-day – here's what your coffee of choice says about your QLC.

ESPRESSO

Crisis Level: Low

There's nothing you love more than efficiency, whether it's for work, your hobbies or getting your daily caffeine hit. You are the envy of those around you, and you are always level-headed in a crisis.

FLAT WHITE

Crisis Level: Low

You feel young at heart so have not yet allowed yourself to enter QLC territory. You're a trendsetter, not a crowd-follower, but if this drink gets any more mainstream, your identity could be called into question.

CAPPUCCINO

Crisis Level: Medium

Though you used to be a positive person, you now find yourself wondering what your purpose in life is at regular intervals during the day. You rely on the warm, frothy milk of your morning caffeine hit for comfort and find you are more sensitive than ever to the opinions of others.

ICED COFFEE

Crisis Level: Medium/High

Just one step away from a Frappuccino, your drink order tells people around you that, yes, you are still young and trendy. You used to be hip and cool, but now you find yourself desperately out of touch with youth culture (i.e. saying things like "hip and cool").

LATTE

Crisis Level: High

You long to order hot milk, but feel pressured to choose the more socially acceptable "latte". You don't particularly like the taste of coffee, so secretly ask for shots of syrup to make the drink more palatable. You'd love a hug from your mama right now.

MOCHA

Crisis Level: High

As you sip something that's little more than a hot chocolate, you find yourself constantly reminiscing about simpler times in your life, when you could curl up in your duvet and watch Netflix all day. Sometimes you still do this anyway.

DOUBLE ESPRESSO

Crisis Level: High

Coffee has become a way to power you through your day while also giving you the impression you're not dying inside. This drink boosts your energy levels to maximum, making it seem like you're enthusiastic about things in your life (which you are very much not).

MATCHA LATTE

Crisis Level: High

You're genuinely not sure what this is, but it's green and all your favourite influencers drink it, so you assume it must be good for you. When you order it, you allow yourself briefly to imagine you are living a different life — specifically one without money worries or extreme job dissatisfaction. Alas, you uncover it is just a drink, and not a magic potion.

Lifesavers

QUARTER-LIFE CRISIS, STEP FIVE:

When you attempt to establish solid coping mechanisms to deal with all the other sh*t going on in your life.

CRAFTING THROUGH YOUR QUARTER-LIFE CRISIS

Rather than grabbing a bottle of wine or CBD-infused water, get crafting instead, and thereby knit, crochet or stitch your way to calmness. There's something rather wonderful about creating a thing of beauty out of the chaos of your quarter-life crisis. It will also serve as a memento when you're old and finally have your sh*t together.

KNIT

Knitting is deeply satisfying, apparently. No, really, it's a chance to zone out and focus fully on a single activity to clear your head. It's also the best way to empty the living room and get control of the TV remote as the constant click-click of needles and occasional "F&%k, I've dropped another stitch!" is enough to drive anyone away. Once you've graduated from a misshapen, holey scarf, just think of all the money you will save when you can make cute accessories for all your got-their-sh*t-together friends' babies.

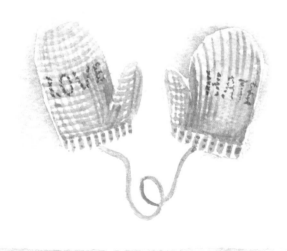

EMBROIDERY

This craft is having a moment, and the kinds of expletive-laden pieces being made these days are not the sort to give to your granny for Christmas. It can be slow-going and require extraordinary patience, but it's heartening to know that you can stab something with precision, multiple times, while immortalizing your favourite swear words using the finest silk thread in a rainbow of colours. Lovely.

CROCHET

This craft requires more brain power than the other two. There's a fair amount of maths involved as you will need to calculate and count constantly to make sure you have the correct amount of stitches. In fact, the maths skills will come in handy when you try to work out how many years it will take you to first pay off your student debt and then save up for a house deposit.

A LIST OF FILMS TO HELP YOU THROUGH THE DARK TIMES OF YOUR QUARTER-LIFE CRISIS

In those moments when you're sorting your taxes or deciding whether to invest in a pension fund, you might feel like wrapping yourself in a burrito blanket and never returning to the light of day again.

Just reach for one of these films and let the quarter-life crises of fictional characters show you that you are not alone – and everything will probably turn out fine in the end.

GOOD WILL HUNTING

What more relatable content could you find than a person who is underpaid, undervalued and misunderstood? This is a film about friendship, dealing with your demons and making the most of life. It's impossible not to feel inspired. And there's a funny joke about blow jobs.

THE DEVIL WEARS PRADA

If you've somehow managed to land that job you always dreamed of, only to realize it is definitely not all it was cracked up to be, then this movie is for you. If you get anything out of this film, let it be that your boss can't be nearly as terrifying as Miranda Priestly. And if they are, run!

THE HARRY POTTER SERIES

Universally loved, these films offer the perfect level of nostalgia value, alongside some serious life lessons. This is a series about growing up, struggling with independence and keeping it together in a terrifying world of goblins, monsters and people dressed in black. Sound familiar?

SLUMDOG MILLIONAIRE

This slumdog underdog fights his way from literal poverty to success. If nothing else, this film will help you to put your own situation in perspective and will give you an overwhelming feel-good feeling at the end.

MEDITATE THE SH*T OUT OF YOUR QUARTER-LIFE CRISIS!

It seems like you can't go anywhere these days without being bashed from behind with a yoga mat by some perfectly coiffed yoga bunny as they rush to the studio to perform 15 downward dogs before their first power meeting of the day. And while you feel shame for leaving your yoga kit drying under your cat, just let those bad vibes go and do something for your mind instead. According to some studies, quarter-lifers are the most stressed demographic the world has ever seen, so be kind to yourself and learn to meditate to reduce stress, encourage emotional balance and make more considered choices. Oh, and the best bit is it's FREE and you can do it ANYWHERE! (Although coffee is always a good accompaniment.) Here's what you need to do:

FIND A PEACEFUL SPOT AND TAKE A SEAT

This is the best excuse you'll ever have to treat yourself to a single-origin flat white in that really nice place with the big comfy booths. Make your own Do Not Disturb sign and place it on the table because you're going to need a good ten minutes' peace to conjure the Zen.

BEGIN WITH A BREATHING EXERCISE

Inhale the delicious coffee aroma for a count of four and then breathe out with a nice big "ahhh". Do this about ten times.

REPEAT A MANTRA

You'll need to get clever for this one. Pop in those earphones so it looks like you're on the phone to someone and say a restorative sentence on repeat for ten minutes, such as "I breathe in calm; I breathe out stress. I am complete." Take a sip of your coffee after every three mantras.

If you feel slightly silly at the prospect of this PDM (public display of meditation), bring a friend – they can get the coffee and you can teach them to meditate. It's win–win.

HELP OTHERS

**What? But I'm having a crisis!
You hear me?
A CRISIS!!!!**

Cool your well-worn boots! I'm sure someone older than you has told you before that there's always somebody out there worse off than you, right? One of the best ways to feel better and gain perspective on your QLC is to help those who are going through tough times too.

BOOST-UP YOUR FELLOW QUARTER-LIFERS

It's been documented that Gen Zers are the loneliest generation ever — even with an average of five gadgets to their name — so why not take the plunge and form a club where you and your fellow quarter-lifers could perhaps knit and natter, or play My Job's Sh*tter Than Yours together.

GET INVOLVED WITH ENVIRONMENTAL CAUSES

If you want to share the good stuff on social networks, then you need to do the good stuff in the first place. Studies show that quarter-lifers may not always have the money to help the cause, but they sure have the enthusiasm. Growing up with digital news 24/7 makes quarter-lifers more aware of the state of the world than any other demographic in history. Use your influence to show you're pro when it comes to environmental causes — it could be an Insta story about litter-picking on the beach, sharing articles about the negative effects of palm oil plantations or you could try out some cruelty-free products on your YouTube channel.

VOLUNTEER FOR A CHARITY

Charity shops and second-hand stores are the go-to places for shoppers with a social conscience. But aside from refreshing your wardrobe, they are great places to volunteer and learn new skills, from visual merchandizing to accounting. Homeless charities are also on the rise, and a few hours of your time will go a long way, such as serving meals in a shelter or organizing a collection of warm blankets and coats.

COMBAT LONELINESS IN YOUR COMMUNITY

Befriend an elderly neighbour and offer to help with their gardening or shopping. Become a companion to the elderly at a day centre or retirement home, or simply make sure you visit the rents a bit more often (without two weeks' worth of laundry) – the thing about parents is they appreciate you so much more when you're just visiting!

THE SABBATICAL

If all else fails and you can't tame or temper the QLC, you need an escape plan.

Some of us still tap the back of the wardrobe to see if we might happen upon a snow-covered land with a hot-looking fawn for company. When those FOMO feelings won't recede, it's time to fly away.

TRAVEL TIPS FOR A QUARTER-LIFE SABBATICAL

So, you've been in the working world for at least a year now (maybe more), and despite a certain element of financial freedom (though probably not enough to move fully out of your parents' house), you've come to the conclusion that working is a total bore. Unless you're one of those lucky few who have landed their dream job by the age of 25, life has probably become an endless cycle of sleep and work (and maybe also attempting to have a social life in between). Maybe it's time to jack it all in for a while and live that gap-year dream. It's time to find yourself or lose yourself – and that must include a beach, a tiny guitar and several dirty Martinis. Here are a few tips for your travels:

PLAN AND PREPARE

Perhaps there's nothing more tempting to you right now than jumping on the next plane to Peru to find out how your avocados grow. But remember that, for many places you want to go, you might need to apply for visas and get vaccinations weeks before you fly. Plan your time before, as well as during, your travel.

PACK A CAMERA, NOT JUST YOUR PHONE... AND A SPARE PAIR OF PANTS

Can you imagine anything worse than trekking all the way to the top of a mountain for the perfect Instagram photo and having your phone die on you? Make sure that you pack a camera, just in case a moment absolutely needs to be captured. #intrepid #alwaysprepared

Plus, the retro wind-on-, old-fashioned-film sort of camera is in fashion these days and will earn you kudos from all those cute hipster backpackers you're going to meet.

LET SOMEONE AT HOME KNOW YOUR PLANS

Especially if you're travelling alone, make sure to let your loved ones know roughly where you're going to be and when. That way, not only will they fret less, but you'll know that someone at home has got your back! Or, go one better and install a tracker on your phone so

Mum and Dad can play at being spies at all hours of the day or night, but be prepared to answer those awks questions like "How come you spent twelve hours in that dodgy bar?" Just say you left your phone there by mistake.

LEARN AND GROW

Chances are at some point you'll have to return to your normal life. Remember to use your experiences to learn about yourself and to grow, such as knowing how to spot the hyenas and dodge the bullets that will inevitably come your way. And all that haggling you did in the market over a cuddly camel will stand you in good stead when you're buying your first home.

The world is your oyster – but it might be a dodgy one, so pack some tablets just to be safe.

FINAL THOUGHTS

What does it really mean to have your sh*t together?

There's nothing more harmful to our well-being than ridiculously high expectations. While some people around you seem to live the perfect life, eating raw kale salads and practising t'ai chi at 5 a.m. every morning before work, this just isn't the way forward for most of us. Sometimes we all need reminding that just keeping vaguely on top of our email inbox and managing to drag a brush through our hair is some pretty great adulting. Here's a list of daily goals for you, to help you get your sh*t together. If you can nail most of these, you're doing great:

☐ You made your bed today.

☐ You cleaned the goop out of the plughole.

☐ You emptied the bin before it overflowed.

☐ You remembered to feed the cat.

☐ You've had a shower in the past 48 hours.

☐ You've spoken to at least one other human.

☐ You ate a square meal.

☐ You brushed your teeth.

☐ You ticked one thing off your to-do list.

Make a reward chart and award yourself a gold star when you have completed each task. Then when you've reached 50 stars, you can give yourself a treat!

TEN COMMANDMENTS FOR THE QUARTER-LIFER

Society seems to have convinced us that "having it all" is the only way for a modern woman to achieve happiness. Frankly, all this achieves is a migraine. Feeling overwhelmed? It's time to adopt a new set of commandments.

1. I WILL SET MY OWN RULES

Contradictory? A bit. But it's important to remember you can follow all of these rules, or none of them, because it's your happiness that's most important.

2. I WILL SAY "NO"

Say no to things that you just really don't want to do, because all you'll achieve by doing them is exhaustion. You do you, boo.

3. I AM COMPLETE REGARDLESS OF MY RELATIONSHIP STATUS

Life is not about scrabbling up the rungs on the relationship ladder until someone puts a ring on it; it's about enjoying the view from where you are. You are already complete.

4. I WILL NOT COMPARE MYSELF TO OTHERS

Your body, intelligence, career accomplishments and relationships are all your own, and are neither greater nor lesser than those of other people around you. Celebrate, don't hate.

5. I WILL HONOUR MY OPINIONS

Make your voice heard and fight for what you believe in, because your opinion is just as important as everyone else's.

6. I WILL LOVE AND RESPECT MY BODY

Not only does your body get you from A to B, but it can do incredible things. Aspire to love and respect your whole being.

7. I WILL IGNORE THE HATERS

In the immortal words of Tay Tay, haters gonna hate. You can't please everyone, so you might as well just try to please yourself.

8. I WON'T SUFFER IN SILENCE

Women are powerhouses, but they are also human. Everyone needs help now and then, so don't be afraid to ask for it.

9. I WILL TAKE LIFE AS IT COMES

Sometimes the brain just has too many tabs open, but overthinking is a sure way to end up with more problems than you started with. Tackle one thing at a time.

10. I WILL CHANNEL MY INNER BEYONCÉ

Let's face it: the world would be a better place if we all summoned our inner Queen Bey. We are all amazing, so let's act like it. Who'll run the world? Girls.

Amen.

MIC DROP

If by the end of this you're still asking when your life will be as perfect as Saint Ariana's, you must remember that if you want things to change, you have to make changes happen – unfortunately "Expecto Patronum" doesn't work in real life (sucks, eh?). This thing called success and having your sh*t together is a lifelong process.

Being a quarter-lifer doesn't mean you should have everything sorted by 25 – if that were the case, the rest of your life would be rather boring and predictable, wouldn't it? It might appear from those dreamy Instagram images that your contemporaries have their #quarterlifegoals in the bag, but the reality is that no one escapes real-life problems and those feelings of loneliness and inadequacy, unless they're a robot (yep, we've all met one or two of those).

So drop-kick that quarter-life crisis and tell it who's boss. One day, when you have older-people problems, you might look back fondly at your quarter-life crisis and wonder, "What the hell was all that about?"

It's time to be kind to yourself and give yourself a pat on the back, because you're doing just fine.

#QUARTERLIFEGOALS

I'm exactly where I need to be.

#QUARTERLIFECRISIS
#QUARTERLIFESKILLS

If you're interested in finding out more about our books, find us on Facebook at Summersdale Publishers and follow us on Twitter at @Summersdale.

www.summersdale.com